D1359603

Welcome to New Zealand

By Patrick Ryan

The Child's World®

Welcome to the WORLD

Published by The Child's World®
1980 Lookout Drive
Mankato, MN 56003-1705
800-599-READ
www.childsworld.com

Content Adviser: Gary Schofield, New Zealand-born writer,
television producer, and artist
Design and Production: The Creative Spark, San Juan, Capistrano, CA
Editorial: Emily J. Dolbear, Brookline, MA
Photo Research: Deborah Goodsite, Califon, NJ

Cover and title page photo: Lawrence Migdale/PIX/www.migdale.com
Interior photos: Alamy: 8 (Mark Boulton), 14 (IML Image Group Ltd), 15 (Nick Servian),
18 (Darroch Donald); AP Photo: 12 (Mark Baker); Corbis: 10 (Stapleton Collection), 19
(Paul A. Souders); Getty Images: 3 top, 13 (Mike Powell/Stone), 27 (Yasuhide Fumoto/Taxi
Japan); Hansen Stock Photos: 11 (Adams); Randall Hyman: 30; iStockphoto.com: 28 (Ufuk
Zivana), 29 (Eva McPherson), 31 (Scott Espie); Landov: 25 (Alessandro Bianchi/Reuters);
NASA Earth Observatory: 4 (Reto Stockli); Panos Pictures: 23 (Jocelyn Carlin); Peter
Arnold, Inc.: 6 (Wolfgang Fuchs/Bilderberg); Photolibrary Group: 22, 24; SuperStock: 3
middle, 7, 9 (Steve Vidler), 3 bottom, 16 (age fotostock), 20 (Steve Vidler).
Map: XNR Productions: 5

Library of Congress Cataloging-in-Publication Data
Ryan, Patrick, 1948–
  Welcome to New Zealand / by Patrick Ryan.
     p. cm. — (Welcome to the world)
  Includes bibliographical references and index.
  ISBN 978-1-59296-973-9 (library bound : alk. paper)
  1. New Zealand—Juvenile literature. I. Title. II. Series.

DU408.R89 2008
993—dc22

2007034774

Contents

Where Is New Zealand?

If you were on a spaceship looking down on Earth, you would see seven large pieces of land called **continents.** Continents can be found all over the planet.

Earth is divided into two halves called **hemispheres.** Australia is one of the continents in the bottom half, or southern hemisphere. Southeast of Australia, there are two large islands. This is the country of New Zealand.

This picture gives us a flat look at Earth. New Zealand is inside the red circle.

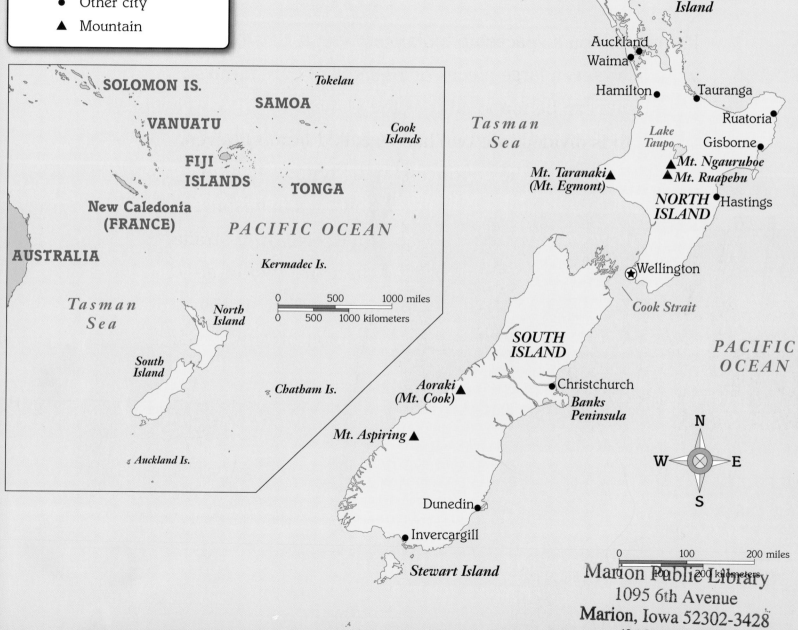

NEW ZEALAND

★ National capital
● Other city
▲ Mountain

Three Kings Islands

Whangarei

Great Barrier Island

Auckland
Waima

Tasman Sea

Hamilton

Tauranga

Ruatoria

Lake Taupo

Gisborne

Mt. Ngauruhoe

Mt. Taranaki
(Mt. Egmont)

Mt. Ruapehu

NORTH ISLAND

Hastings

Wellington

Cook Strait

SOUTH ISLAND

Christchurch
Banks Peninsula

PACIFIC OCEAN

Aoraki
(Mt. Cook)

Mt. Aspiring

Dunedin

Invercargill

Stewart Island

N W E S

Inset map

SOLOMON IS.
Tokelau
SAMOA
VANUATU
Cook Islands
FIJI ISLANDS
TONGA
New Caledonia (FRANCE)
PACIFIC OCEAN
AUSTRALIA
Kermadec Is.
Tasman Sea
North Island
0 500 1000 miles
0 500 1000 kilometers
South Island
Chatham Is.
Auckland Is.

0 100 200 miles
0 100 200 kilometers

The Land

New Zealand is made up of two main parts—the North Island and the South Island. There are also many smaller islands, but not many people live there. One thing that you are sure to find in New Zealand is mountains. They can be found almost everywhere.

Mount Ngauruhoe is located on the North Island in Tongariro National Park. It's an active volcano!

On the North Island, there is rich farmland and green forests. There are also volcanoes. Some of them still erupt! The South Island is larger than the North Island. It also has thick forests and tall mountains. In fact, some 20 mountains on South Island are more than 10,000 feet (3,048 meters) high. They are called the Southern Alps.

Sheep graze in a field in the Southern Alps.

Plants and Animals

New Zealand could be called the land of mysterious plants. That's because more than 2,000 kinds, or **species,** grow there. About 1,500 of these cannot be found anywhere else in the world. Mamaku and wheki-ponga plants, or tree ferns, grow in many places. New Zealand has kauri, rimu, and totara trees, too.

A tall kauri tree grows in North Island's Waipoua Forest.

Many animals in New Zealand started out as visitors. They were brought to the islands many years ago by settlers from other continents. Deer, weasels, opossums, and rabbits all came to New Zealand with new settlers on their boats. But a dinosaur-like animal has been roaming New Zealand for millions of years! It's called a tuatara.

Did you know?

New Zealand's most famous bird cannot fly! Kiwi birds (left) make their homes in the green forests of the islands. They have long beaks and a good sense of smell.

Long Ago

According to legend, an explorer named Kupe was the first to discover New Zealand. Kupe arrived by canoe sometime around the year 900. He was a member of a group of people called the Maori (MAU-ree). The early Maori people were warriors who traveled by canoe. They were highly organized

This engraving shows Maori people traveling by canoe.

and skilled in many crafts. The Maori liked the islands and settled there.

In 1642, a Dutch explorer named Abel Tasman saw New Zealand's islands from his ship. He found the land beautiful, but he did not go ashore because he was afraid of the Maori! Finally British explorer Captain James Cook

This statue of Captain James Cook overlooks New Zealand's port of Gisborne.

arrived in 1769 and opened the islands to be settled. By 1840, New Zealand was part of the **British Empire.**

Britain's Prince William poses with children for a group photograph during a visit to New Zealand in 2005.

New Zealand Today

Today, New Zealand has its own government, laws, and rules as well as its own flag. Even so, New Zealand still has close ties with the country of England. In fact, New Zealand recognizes the Queen of England as one of its official leaders.

The Maori people contribute much to New Zealand society. Many Maori help make laws and rules that protect their native peoples and lands. They also work hard to protect New Zealand and the many plants and animals that live there. Both Maori and European cultures play an important role in the success of New Zealand. The future of the country depends on both cultures.

In the traditional Maori greeting called *hongi*, two people press their noses together. Here a Maori man greets a tourist.

The People

About 4 million people live in New Zealand. Most of them live on the North Island. Most everyone in New Zealand lives on or near a coast. Many New Zealanders are relatives of the early settlers and explorers from other countries. Others belong to the Maori people.

A Maori woman holds her daughter. They live in the small North Island town of Ruatoria.

New Zealanders of various backgrounds wait at a Wellington bus stop together.

Many **immigrants** also live in New Zealand. They are people who moved from other countries to live in New Zealand. Many immigrants come to New Zealand from the Pacific Islands, India, China, and Vietnam.

The city of Auckland is on the North Island.

City Life and Country Life

Most of New Zealand's people live in cities. Auckland and Wellington are the two big cities on the North Island. Christchurch and Dunedin are the big cities on the South Island. Wellington is the capital city of the country. It is located on the coast between the two islands.

New Zealand's cities have busy streets full of buildings, shops, restaurants, and hotels. City people live in houses or apartments called flats. Many drive cars or ride buses to go places.

The countryside of New Zealand is much calmer. The people there live on small farms or in little towns. Many people raise sheep in the large fields. In fact, New Zealand is home to more than 40 million sheep!

Reputedly known as the longest place name in the world

TAUMATAWHAKATANGI HANGAKOAUAUOTAMATEA TURIPUKAKAPIKIMAUNGA HORONUKUPOKAIWHEN UAKITANATAHU

THE PLACE WHERE TAMATEA, THE MAN WITH THE BIG KNEES, WHO SLID, CLIMBED, AND SWALLOWED MOUNTAINS, KNOWN AS LANDEATER, PLAYED HIS FLUTE TO HIS LOVED ONE.

Guinness Book of Records

A Maori road sign points to a hill in New Zealand with one of the world's longest place names.

Schools and Language

Children in New Zealand start school when they are about five or six years old. Some start as young as three years old. Young students learn math, reading, and writing. At some schools, students must wear uniforms. The country also has excellent libraries and universities.

New Zealand has three official languages— English, Maori, and New Zealand Sign Language. The Maori language is used in ceremonies and special occasions. Some Maori words can even be found in English. *Kiwi* is one Maori word that many people use in everyday life.

Students from the village of Waima read together during an outdoor lesson.

New Zealand farmers buy and sell livestock at a public sale.

Work

New Zealanders work at many different jobs. Some people work in the cities at big companies. Others work in restaurants or small shops. Farming and raising animals in New Zealand are very important jobs, too. The mild weather is perfect for growing crops and raising huge herds of sheep and cows.

Another important job in New Zealand is **tourism.** In this job, New Zealanders show visitors from other places around the country. They show people their beautiful forests, wild animals, and busy cities. Each year, more and more travelers come to New Zealand to enjoy its natural beauty and clean air, land, and water.

Food

New Zealanders enjoy many of the same foods that we do. They also have many interesting dishes of their own. Many New Zealanders like to eat tea and cookies, or biscuits, in the middle of the afternoon.

A New Zealand lamb with roasted vegetables

Many people in New Zealand like to eat roasted **mutton,** or lamb. It is used in lots of dishes, from soup to sandwiches. Another favorite dish is the meat pie. It has a flaky crust and is filled with meat or vegetables.

Customers eat at a café near a large sculpture of a kiwi on the edge of South Island.

Downhill skiing is a popular vacation pastime in New Zealand.

Pastimes

The New Zealand All Blacks gather before the start of a rugby match.

There is one word for sports in New Zealand—rugby. New Zealanders love to play it and watch it, too. The national New Zealand rugby team is called the All Blacks. They get their name from the fact that they wear all black uniforms. They are considered one of the best rugby teams in the world.

When they are not playing rugby, many people spend time doing other things outdoors. New Zealanders often go hiking, camping, skiing, and snowboarding in the mountains. At the sea, people fish, swim, and sail.

Holidays

New Zealanders have many holidays special to their country. They celebrate their national day on February 6. New Zealanders honor the people who fought during the two world wars on April 25. At the beginning of June, they celebrate the Queen of England's birthday.

New Zealand is a wonderful country full of unusual plants and towering mountains. Its beautiful countryside and mild weather make it a perfect vacation spot. The people of New Zealand are happy and kind—and they are ready for you to come and visit one day!

Did you know?

The seasons take place at opposite times in Earth's hemispheres. The northern hemisphere enjoys springtime while the southern hemisphere prepares for winter. That's why New Zealanders celebrate Christmas in the middle of their summer!

Sisters wearing their school uniforms prepare to play soccer.

Area: 103,738 square miles (268,680 square kilometers)—about the size of Colorado

Population: About 4 million people

Capital City: Wellington

Other Important Cities: Auckland, Christchurch, Hamilton, and Dunedin

Money: The New Zealand dollar

National Language: English, Maori, and New Zealand Sign Language (added in 2006)

National Holiday: Waitangi Day on February 6 (1840)

National Flag: Blue with the flag of the United Kingdom in the upper left corner. There are also four white-edged red stars on the flag. They represent a group of real stars in the night sky called the Southern Cross.

Head of State: The governor general of New Zealand

Head of Government: The prime minister of New Zealand

Famous People:

Jane Campion: film director

Bernard Freyberg: general

Sir Edmund Hillary: explorer

Peter Jackson: film director

Rowena Othlie Jackson: ballet dancer

Katherine Mansfield: short-story writer

Sam Neill: actor

Anna Paquin: actor

Ernest Rutherford: winner of the Nobel Prize in Chemistry in 1908

Jenny Shipley: first female prime minister, from 1997 to 1999

Kiri Te Kanawa: opera singer

Hone Tuwhare: poet

National Song: New Zealand has two national songs: "God Defend New Zealand" and "God Save the Queen (or King)."

"God Defend New Zealand"

God of nations, at Thy feet
In the bonds of love we meet.
Hear our voices, we entreat,
God defend our free land.
Guard Pacific's triple star
From the shafts of strife and
      war.
Make her praises heard afar,
God defend New Zealand.

Men of every creed and race
Gather here before Thy face,
Asking Thee to bless this place,
God defend our free land.
From dissension, envy, hate

And corruption guard our state,
Make our country good and
      great,
God defend New Zealand.
Peace, not war, shall be our
      boast,
But, should foes assail our
      coast,
Make us then a mighty host,
God defend our free land.
Lord of battles, in Thy might,
Put our enemies to flight,
Let our cause be just and right,
God defend New Zealand.

Let our love for Thee increase,
May Thy blessings never cease,

Give us plenty, give us peace,
God defend our free land.
From dishonor and from shame
Guard our country's spotless
      name,
Crown her with immortal fame,
God defend New Zealand.

May our mountains ever be
Freedom's ramparts on the sea,
Make us faithful unto Thee,
God defend our free land.
Guide her in the nations' van,
Preaching love and truth to
      man,
Working out Thy glorious plan,
God defend New Zealand.

"God Save the Queen (or King)"

God save our gracious Queen,
Long live our noble Queen,
God save the Queen!
Send her victorious,
Happy and Glorious,
Long to reign over us;
God save the Queen!

O Lord our God arise,
Scatter her enemies
And make them fall;
Confound their politics,

Frustrate their knavish tricks,
On Thee our hopes we fix,
God, save us all!

Thy choicest gifts in store
On her be pleased to pour;
Long may she reign;
May she defend our laws,
And ever give us cause
To sing with heart and voice,
God save the Queen!

29

How Do You Say...

ENGLISH	MAORI	HOW TO SAY IT
hello	kia ora	KEE or-ah
good-bye	haere rä	HIGH-re rah
please	koa	KO-ah
thank you	kia ora	KEE or-ah
one	tahi	TA-hee
two	rua	ROO-ah
three	toru	TOH-roo
New Zealand	Aotearoa	ah-OH-te-ah-row-ah

Glossary

British Empire (BRIH-tish EM-pire)
Colonies that belonged to England were part of the British Empire. New Zealand became part of the British Empire in 1840.

continents (KON-tih-nents) All the land areas on Earth are divided up into huge sections called continents. Most of the continents are separated by oceans.

hemispheres (HEM-iss-feers)
Earth is divided into two halves called hemispheres. New Zealand is in the southern hemisphere.

immigrants (IM-ih-grents) Immigrants are people who move to a country from somewhere else.

mutton (MUH-tun) Mutton is meat from sheep. Many New Zealand dishes are made with mutton.

species (SPEE-sheez) A species is a group of similar plants or animals. There are more than 2,000 species of plants in New Zealand.

tourism (TOOR-ih-zum) The business of showing travelers around a country is called tourism. Tourism is an important source of jobs in New Zealand.

Further Information

Read It

Coburn, Broughton. *Triumph on Everest: A Photobiography of Sir Edmund Hillary.* Washington, DC: National Geographic Children's Books, 2003.

Di Piazza, Francesca. *New Zealand in Pictures.* Minneapolis: Twenty-First Century Books, 2005.

Mattern, Joanne. *Crazy Creatures of Australia and New Zealand.* Logan, IA: Perfection Learning, 2001.

Theunissen, Steve. *The Maori of New Zealand.* Minneapolis: Lerner Publications Co., 2002.

Look It Up

Visit our Web page for lots of links about New Zealand:
http://www.childsworld.com/links

Note to Parents, Teachers, and Librarians: We routinely verify our Web links to make sure they are safe, active sites—so encourage your readers to check them out!

Index